THIS BOOK BELONGS TO...

Name:	Age:

Favourite player:

2019/2020

My Predictions...	Actual...
Town's final position:	
Town's top scorer:	
League One Winners:	
League One top scorer:	
FA Cup Winners:	
EFL Cup Winners:	

Contributors: Peter Rogers

A TWOCAN PUBLICATION

ISBN 978-1-911502-73-9

PICTURE CREDITS: Dan Sakal & Warren Page, Grant Pringle, Action Images and Press Association.

£9

adidas
MAGICAL
VEGAS

CONTENTS

Tomas **HOLY**

01

POSITION: Goalkeeper **COUNTRY:** Czech Republic **DOB:** 10 December 1991

Giant Czech goalkeeper Tomas Holy joined Ipswich Town in the summer of 2019 on a free transfer. He had gained an excellent reputation following a two-and-a-half year spell with Gillingham. His League One experience gained with the Gills is sure to be a great asset as he competes to be first choice 'keeper at Portman Road for the 2019/20 season.

Janoi **DONACIEN**

POSITION: Defender **COUNTRY:** St Lucia **DOB:** 3 November 1993

Having begun his career at Aston Villa, defender Janoi Donacien gained valuable experience with loan spells at Tranmere Rovers, Wycombe Wanderers and Newport County before sealing a permanent move to Accrington Stanley. He joined Ipswich in the summer of 2018. Initially arriving on loan, the deal became permanent once a work permit had been granted. He spent the second half of 2018/19 back on loan at Stanley and will be keen to make his mark with Town at League One level.

Luke CHAMBERS 04

POSITION: Defender **COUNTRY:** England **DOB:** 28 September 1985

Club captain and 2018/19 Player of the Year, Luke Chambers agreed a new contract with the club in the final weeks of last season and the skipper will be keen to play a major role in leading the club back to the Championship. Signed from Nottingham Forest back in 2012, Chambers has become a consistent presence at the heart of the Town defence where his brave and committed performances have seen him recognised as a firm fans' favourite.

THE 2019/20 SQUAD

James WILSON 05

POSITION: Defender **COUNTRY:** Wales **DOB:** 26 February 1989

After training with Town during the pre-season period, experienced central defender James Wilson agreed a short-term deal at Portman Road keeping him at the club initially until the end of 2019. A full Welsh international, Wilson made his debut in Town's opening day victory away to Burton Albion. With good knowledge of the League One scene, Wilson is sure to be a valuable asset to Paul Lambert's squad.

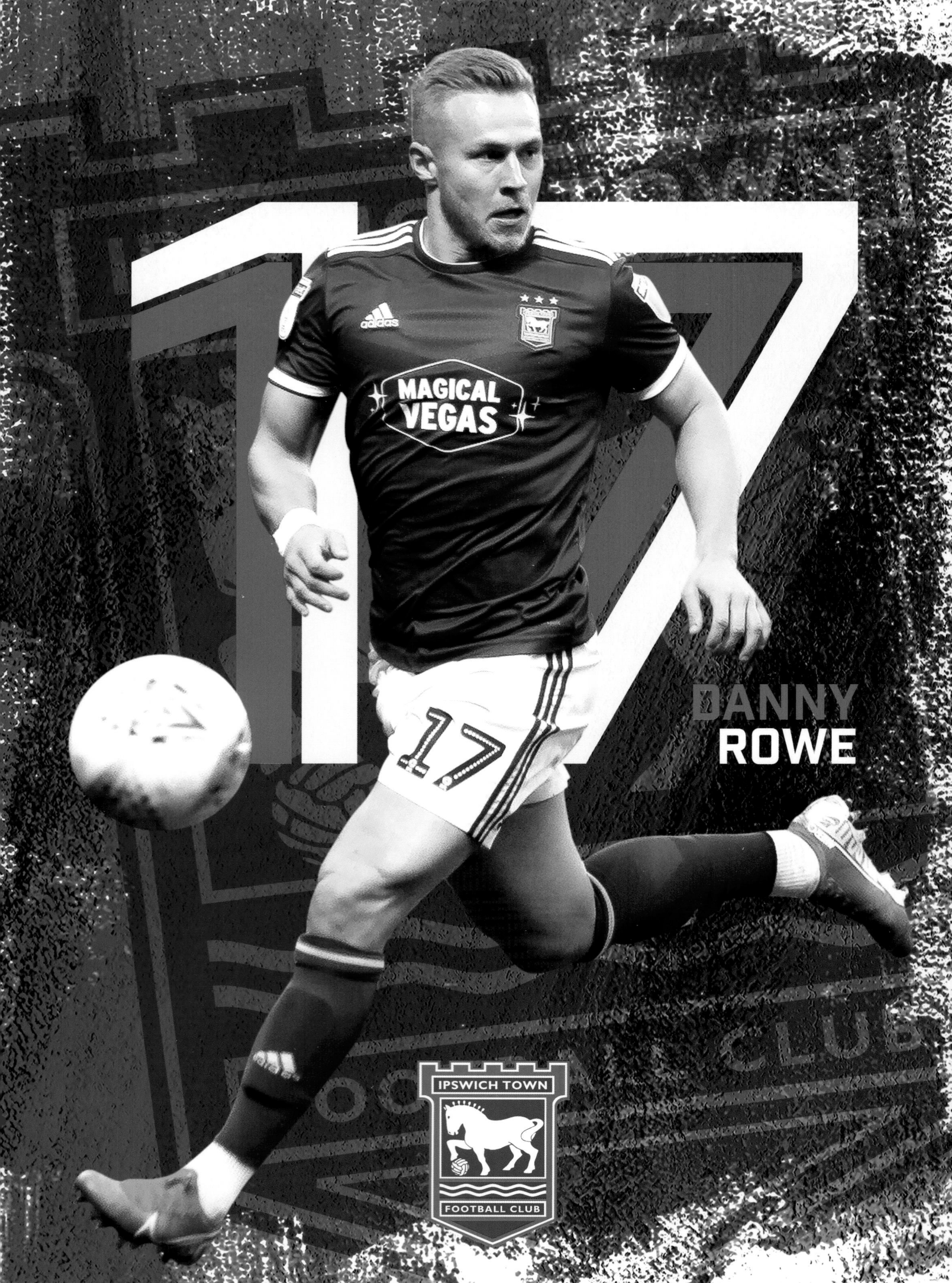
DANNY
ROWE
MAGICAL
VEGAS
IPSWICH TOWN
FOOTBALL CLUB

THE LEGEND MICK MILLS

Aged just 17, full-back Mick Mills made the first of his record 741 Ipswich appearances as Town recorded a comprehensive 5-2 Second Division victory over Wolves at Portman Road in May 1966. From that historic moment, Mills made a further 740 appearances over a 16-year period as the club enjoyed its greatest spell of success.

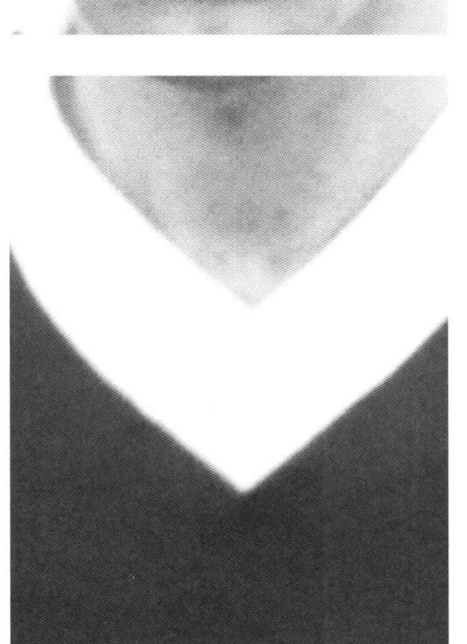

After spending his late teens establishing himself on the first-team scene at Portman Road, Mills achieved the first of his many triumphs with the club in 1968 as Town won promotion to the old First Division. The 1968/69 season saw Town crowned Second Division champions as they held off a strong challenge from QPR to take the title.

Following the arrival of Bobby Robson as the club's manager, Mills soon impressed his new boss and the reliable full-back was named Ipswich Town captain in 1971. Mills took great pride in captaining the side and in 1972/73 Town finished fourth in the top flight and won the Texaco Cup.

On Saturday, 6 May 1978 Mick Mills became the first, and to-date only, Ipswich Town captain to hold aloft the FA Cup. Town were underdogs when they faced Arsenal in the Wembley showpiece. However, a single goal from Roger Osborne and a resolute defensive display saw Mills lead his men up the famous Wembley steps to collect the cup on a never-to-be-forgotten day in Ipswich's rich history.

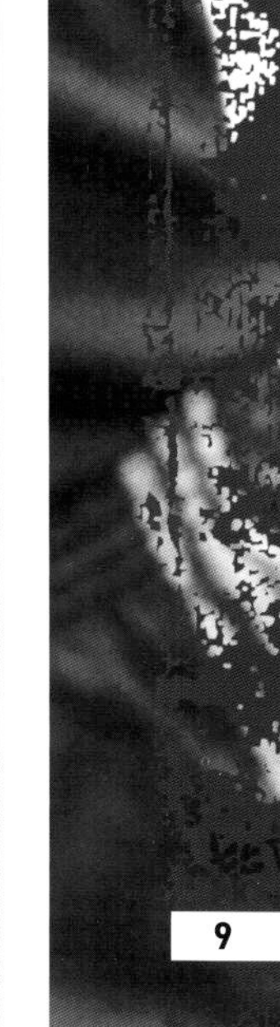

During the club's halcyon days under Bobby Robson, Town were consistent First Division title challengers. In 1980/81 they ended the campaign as runners-up. Despite that league title near-miss, Mills and his teammates railed to end the season on a positive note by winning the UEFA Cup. Over a two-legged final against AZ Alkmaar, Town ran out 5-4 winners and Mills was presented with the trophy on an unforgettable evening in Amsterdam.

FREDDIE SEARS

2018/19

GOAL OF THE SEASON

Freddie Sears' goal at Aston Villa on 26 January 2019 was named the Ipswich Town Goal of the Season for 2018/19 at the club's official end-of-season dinner event.

With 76 minutes on the clock at Villa Park, Sears lashed home from the edge of the box after a well-worked passing move from deep in the Blues' own half. It really was a venomous strike which left Villa 'keeper Lovre Kalinic helpless. Unsurprisingly the goal was also voted the EFL's Championship Goal of the Month for January. Sears' effort pulled the scoreline back to 2-1 but Town, who were denied a very strong shout for a penalty, were unable to take a point from the game.

Such a high quality strike was a fitting reward from what was widely regarded as one of Town's most impressive away performances of the season. The Blues' Villa Park display was certainly worthy of a share of the spoils as Paul Lambert's men provided tough opposition against one of his former clubs.

Without a goal until Lambert's arrival as boss, Sears produced an impressive run of goalscoring form by hitting four goals in Lambert's first four matches at the helm. Sadly, just two games after his Villa Park wonder-strike, Sears suffered a cruciate ligament injury in the East Anglian derby defeat at Norwich which ended his season and was expected to sideline him for around nine months.

A fully fit Sears during the 2019/20 season will certainly be like a new signing for Town. All at Portman Road hope to see him back in action and banging in the goals again just like he did at Villa Park!

THE CONTENDERS

There were several contenders for the prestigious award with Kayden Jackson's impressive New Year's Day strike against Millwall, plus Andre Dozzell finishing off a great team move against Leeds United on the final day of the season being serious rivals to Sears' super strike.

THE 2019/20 SQUAD

Gwion EDWARDS 07

POSITION: Midfielder COUNTRY: Wales DOB: 1 March 1993

Welsh wideman Gwion Edwards moved from Peterborough United to Portman Road in the summer of 2018 after agreeing a two-year deal with Town. The midfielder wasted little time in making his mark with the Tractor Boys as he opened the scoring just five minutes into his debut as Town drew 2-2 with Blackburn Rovers on the opening day of the season. He further adhered himself to the Portman Road crowd by slamming the ball home to give Ipswich the lead in the first East Anglian derby of the season in September 2018.

Cole SKUSE 08

POSITION: Midfielder COUNTRY: England DOB: 29 March 1986

A vastly experienced midfielder, Cole Skuse joined Ipswich Town in the summer of 2013 after making over 300 first team appearances for Bristol City. A loyal servant to the Robins and now to Town, Skuse had played approaching 250 games for the Blues as at the end of 2018/19. As Town now look to develop a number of their exciting young players, Skuse's experience and knowhow are sure to be a great benefit to those around him in the Blues' midfield engine room.

Kayden JACKSON 09

POSITION: Striker **COUNTRY:** England **DOB:** 22 February 1994

A star performer with 16 goals for Accrington Stanley in their 2017/18 League Two title-winning campaign, striker Kayden Jackson joined Ipswich Town in August 2018. A powerful and robust frontman, Jackson netted his first goal for the Blues in the League Cup match with Exeter City and opened his Championship account with a second-half equaliser at home to Brentford in September 2018.

James NORWOOD 10

POSITION: Striker **COUNTRY:** England **DOB:** 24 October 1990

Ipswich Town's marquee signing ahead of their 2019/20 League One campaign, striker James Norwood arrived at Portman Road after helping Tranmere Rovers win promotion from League Two via the 2018/19 Play-Offs. A proven goalscorer with Forest Green and at Prenton Park, Norwood will be Town's go-to man for goals as they look to make their mark in League One.

D Wears the Birmingham City captain's armband

Crystal Palace's nickname E

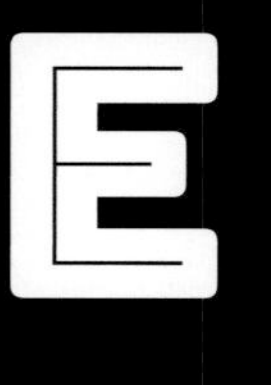

Skipper of League One new boys, the Imps F

A Chelsea's Spanish skipper

B

Do you recognise this League One club's crest

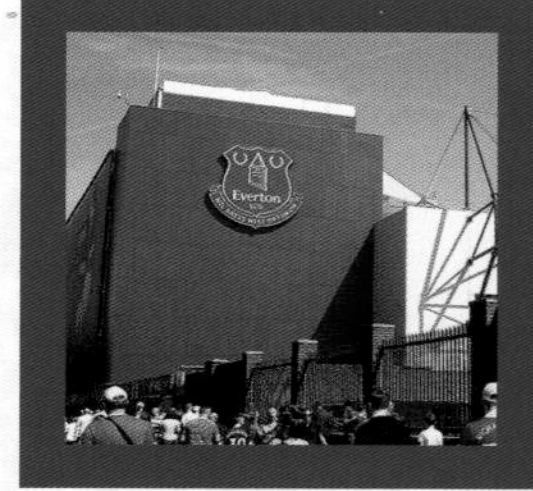

The Toffees play their home games here G

H Longest serving Championship manager and a Millwall legend

Scored the first home league goal of the season at the City Ground C

I Foxes' Nigeria international signing who wears No.8

A-Z 2019/20 PART 1

WHO'S WHO & WHAT'S WHAT OF ENGLISH FOOTBALL?

J

Manchester City's Brazilian striker who was part of their 2019 Copa América winning side

L

This England international has been with the Red Devils since the age of 7

K

Polish international midfielder who was ever-present for Leeds United last season

M

Former WBA player and manager, now in the Doncaster Rovers hot-seat

ANSWERS ON PAGE 62

AT THE TRAINING GROUND...

Come three o'clock on a Saturday afternoon, the fans get to see their heroes in action at Portman Road.

Matchday is the day the Blues' players, manager and coaching staff are all preparing for and focusing on throughout the week. All that preparation takes places at the club's training ground, well away from the watching eyes of the thousands of fans who flock to Portman Road in hope of witnessing another winning performance.

The hard work begins in the summer months when the players all report back for pre-season training. The players are given a fitness programme to follow over the summer break and the first few days back at the training ground tend to involve a number of fitness tests. The results will enable Paul Lambert's coaching and fitness staff to assess each player's condition and level of fitness to ensure they are given the right workload over pre-season, so that they are fully match fit and raring to go for the big kick-off.

A lot of the work done over the pre-season period is designed to help the players reach a level of fitness that they can maintain for the entire campaign and perform at their maximum throughout the season.

When it comes to winning football matches, it is well known that practice, dedication and preparation are all vital ingredients for success. However, in terms of strength and fitness; rest, recovery and diet also play crucial parts in a footballer's welfare. The Ipswich Town players are not only given the best of surfaces to practice on, but also given expert advice and guidance to ensure that they are fully equipped for the League One challenges ahead.

Technology also plays its part in helping the Ipswich stars perform to their maximum. Prior to taking to the training pitches, players are provided with a GPS tracking system and heart rate analysis monitors ensuring that all they do, can be measured, monitored and reviewed.

And if all goes to plan, the team's drive, commitment and meticulous preparation on the training ground during the week, will pay dividends on matchday.

IPSWICH TOWN
FOOTBALL CLUB
adidas

THE LEGEND ALAN BRAZIL

Scottish striker Alan Brazil began his goalscoring career at Ipswich Town in the late 1970s. His first team breakthrough arrived when Bobby Robson handed him his professional debut in the club's 1977/78 First Division campaign. Brazil's debut came against the mighty Manchester United at Portman Road on Saturday, 14 January 1978. Although the match ended in a defeat it marked a significant moment in Brazil's playing career.

Brazil's debut may have been tinged by the fact that Town suffered a 2-1 defeat to Manchester United back in 1978, but come the 1979/80 season and Brazil was a first choice starter and very much a man in form. He opened the scoring against Manchester United after just two minutes on 1 March 1980. On what became a memorable afternoon at Portman Road, Brazil added another while strike partner Paul Mariner netted a hat-trick as Town thrashed United 6-0.

Striker Brazil added his name to the list of goalscorers in Town's triumphant 1980/81 UEFA Cup run. On a night when John Wark grabbed the headlines with a hat-trick, Brazil scored Town's vital second goal just before the break in the third round meeting with Widzew Lodz. Town went on to register a 5-0 victory in this first-leg match against the Polish side on 26 November 1980.

Alan Brazil enjoyed one of his greatest achievements with Ipswich Town as Bobby Robson's men conquered AZ Alkmaar in the 1980/81 UEFA Cup final. Brazil partnered Paul Mariner in both legs of the final as Ipswich ran out 5-4 winners and lifted the trophy in Amsterdam on 20 May 1981.

One of Alan Brazil's finest games in a Town shirt came on Tuesday, 16 February 1982 when he scored all five goals in Town's 5-2 First Division demolition of Southampton at Portman Road. The popular Scot displayed a devastating display of clinical finishing that is still fondly recalled by the Portman Road faithful.

23
ANDRE
DOZZELL
MAGICAL
VEGAS
adidas
IPSWICH TOWN
FOOTBALL CLUB

IPSWICH TOWN
FOOTBALL CLUB
EMPIRE
EMPIRE
#PEAKE
24
For all you   ontaine Haulage ne

IPSWICH TOWN WOMEN

Following the outstanding performances of England's Lionesses in the 2019 Women's World Cup finals in France, participation and interest in the women's game continues to grow at a rapid pace. Town's own women's team will certainly be looking to take a level of inspiration from the Lionesses' summer achievements when their new 2019/20 season gets underway.

Fixtures for the new Women's National League season will see the Blues begin their campaign at home to AFC Wimbledon. The Tractor Girls will host the Dons at the Goldstar Ground on Sunday, 18 August before travelling to face newly promoted Kent Football United for their first away trip on Sunday, 1 September.

Town will face an early encounter with local rivals Norwich City, with the first East Anglian Derby set to take place on Wednesday, 4 September at the Goldstar Ground. The Canaries will host the reverse fixture on Wednesday, 19 February.

The first Derby game will be the first of two midweek games for the Blues in 2019 as Joe Sheehan's side also play host to recently promoted Cambridge City on Wednesday, 9 October. Town will finish the calendar year at home to Cambridge United on Sunday, 8 December.

2020 begins with a rematch of the opening day fixture as the Blues travel to South-West London to face AFC Wimbledon on Sunday, 12 January before hosting Kent Football United on Sunday, 2 February.

After the final East Anglian Derby of the season on 19 February, the Tractor Girls have one remaining midweek fixture at Cambridge City on Wednesday, 18 March. The Blues' final home game against Stevenage takes place on Sunday, 29 March before the league campaign concludes away at Cambridge United on Sunday, 10 May.

For all the latest news on The Tractor Girls log on to www.itfcwomen.co.uk or follow them on twitter @itfcwomen

Jon
NOLAN

11

POSITION: Midfielder **COUNTRY: England** **DOB: 22 November 1982**

Jon Nolan followed his former boss Paul Hurst from Shrewsbury Town to Portman Road in the summer of 2018. A technically gifted player, whose performances for the promotion-seeking Shrews in 2017/18 won him many admirers. He netted three goals during his debut season with Town to help the team earn points from their Championship clashes with Birmingham City, Derby County and West Bromwich Albion.

Will
NORRIS

12

POSITION: Goalkeeper **COUNTRY: England** **DOB: 13 August 1993**

Goalkeeper Will Norris joined Town on a season-long loan deal from Premier League Wolverhampton Wanderers on the eve of the new 2019/20 season. Norris turned professional with Cambridge United before earning his move to Molineux in the summer of 2017. Due to the form of initially John Ruddy and subsequently Rui Patricio, Norris has been limited to mainly cup action but made his Premier League bow in Wolves' final home game of 2018/19.

Jack
LANKESTER

14

POSITION: Striker **COUNTRY:** England **DOB:** 19 January 2000

Academy graduate Jack Lankester capped off a memorable 2018/19 season by breaking through to the first team and winning the Dale Roberts Academy Player of the Year award. Lankester debuted in Town's home match with QPR in October 2018 and added his name to the score sheet in the New Year's Day clash with Millwall. With emphasis firmly on youth at Portman Road, Lankester will be hopeful of further opportunities to showcase his talents in 2019/20.

THE 2019/20 SQUAD

Teddy
BISHOP

POSITION: Midfielder **COUNTRY:** England **DOB:** 15 July 1996

Teddy Bishop joined the Ipswich Town Academy as an eight-year-old and has progressed through the age groups to make his mark on the first-team scene. A creative player who loves to get on the ball and be the spark to switch defence to attack, Bishop possesses a great range of passing skills. Injury sidelined him from the start of the 2019/20 season but he will be keen to make a positive impression on the club's League One campaign once fully fit.

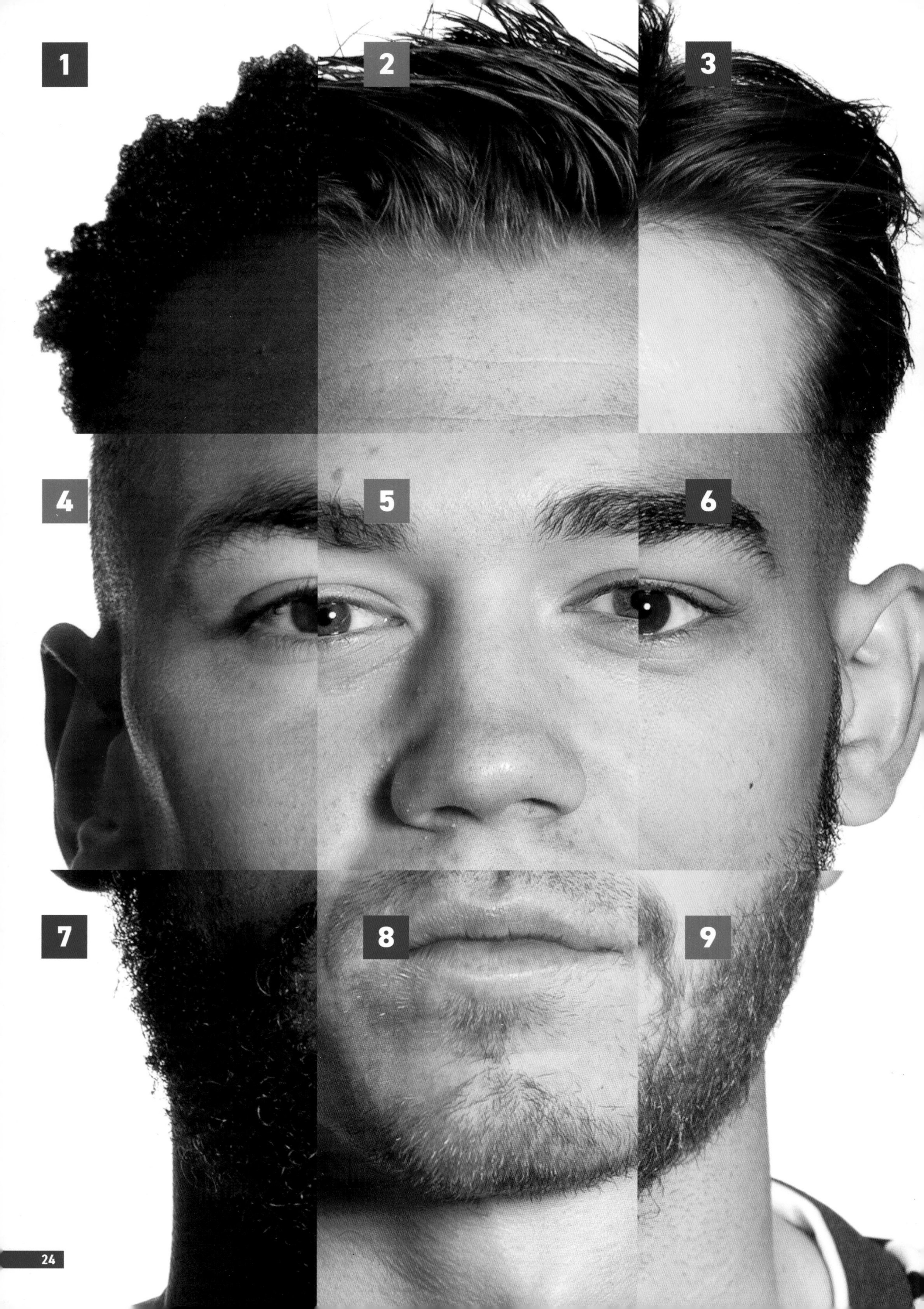
1
2
3
4
5
6
7
8
9

10

11

Can you figure out who these Blues stars are?

12

WHO ARE YER

13

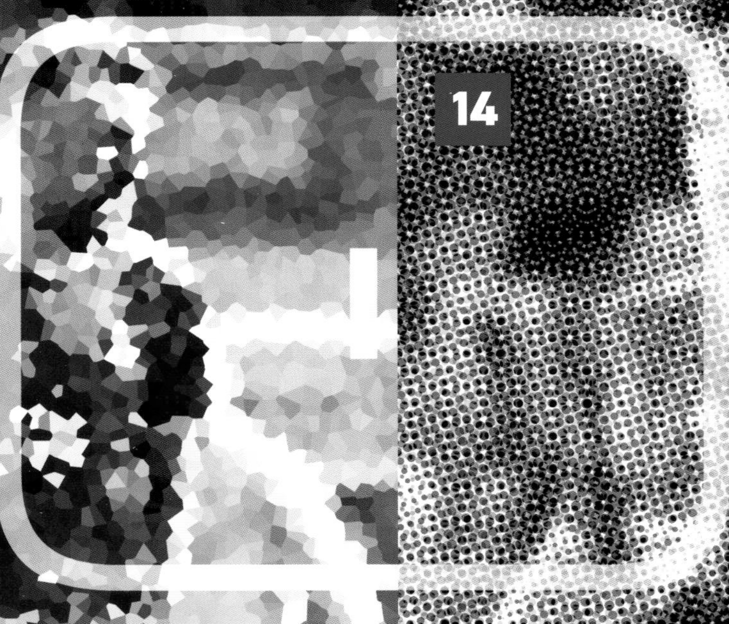

14

ANSWERS ON PAGE 62

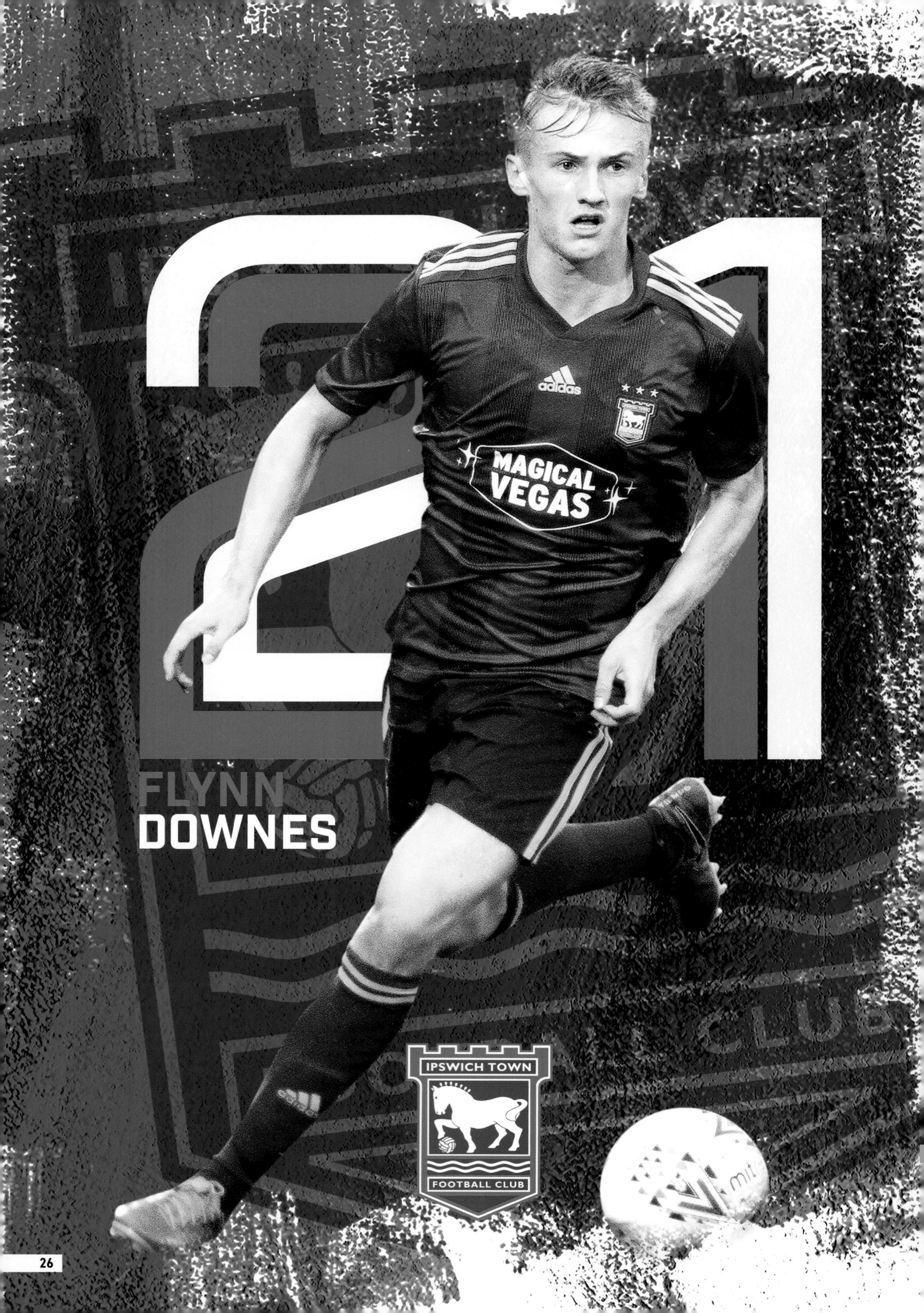
21
FLYNN
DOWNES
adidas
MAGICAL
VEGAS
IPSWICH TOWN
FOOTBALL CLUB

Colour me!
MYLES KENLOCK 30
IPSWICH TOWN
FOOTBALL CLUB
MAGICAL VEGAS

Tristan NYDAM

16

POSITION: Midfielder **COUNTRY:** England **DOB:** 6 November 1999

An England youth international, Tristan Nydam can play at left-back or in a midfield role and has been capped at Under-18 and Under-19 level by the Three Lions. After breaking through from the club's academy to the first team in 2017/18, he was loaned to Scottish Premiership club St Johnstone for the first half of the 2018/19 season. Opportunities were limited at McDiarmid Park and Nydam returned to Portman Road in January 2019.

Danny ROWE

17

POSITION: Midfielder **COUNTRY:** England **DOB:** 9 March 1992

Plucked from then non-league Macclesfield Town in January 2017 by Mick McCarthy, midfielder Danny Rowe put pen to paper on the three-and-a-half year deal at Portman Road. Rowe spent the majority of the 2017/18 season on loan at League Two Lincoln City and tasted EFL Trophy success with the Imps at Wembley. The 2018/19 campaign saw him feature in both of Paul Lambert's first two games in charge before returning to Sincil Bank on loan for the remainder of the campaign.

Alan JUDGE 18

POSITION: Midfielder **COUNTRY:** Republic of Ireland **DOB:** 11 November 1988

Experienced Republic of Ireland international midfielder Alan Judge arrived at Portman Road from Brentford in January 2019. The midfield playmaker soon added a touch of class to the Town side and despite relegation the Irishman put pen to paper on a new two-year deal with the club in April 2019. His undoubted ability is sure to be a great asset to Town in their 2019/20 League One campaign.

THE 2019/20 SQUAD

Jordan ROBERTS 19

POSITION: Midfielder **COUNTRY:** England **DOB:** 5 January 1994

Winger Jordan Roberts left Crawley Town in July 2018 to try his luck at Championship level with Town. Paul Lambert named Roberts in his first Ipswich team and he made a positive impression in the 1-1 draw with Preston at Portman Road in November 2018. He remained in the first team frame until the turn of the year when Town recruited the experienced Collin Quaner and Will Keane on loan to lead the line in Town's battle for Championship survival. Roberts then ended last season with a loan spell at Lincoln City.

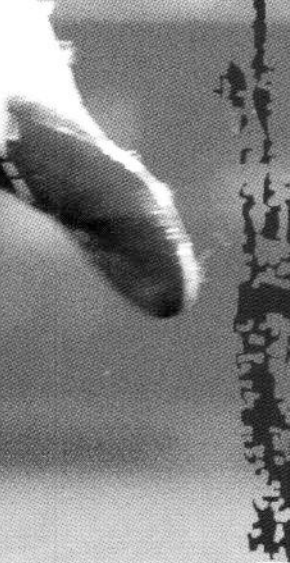

The second half of the 2018/19 season saw a number of improved performances under new boss Paul Lambert as Town battled bravely for Championship survival. Here are three to remember...

REWIND

IPSWICH TOWN 1 ROTHERHAM UNITED 0

Town displayed a resolute defensive performance to begin the calendar year of 2019 at Portman Road with a win. The Blues bounced back from the disappointment of their FA Cup exit at Accrington the previous week to defeat Rotherham United 1-0.

The home defence was marshalled expertly by Wales international debutant James Collins who produced an assured performance. Collins headed, blocked and stopped all that the Millers could offer, while his presence and experience clearly had a positive effect on those around him.

While Collins did his work in the defensive areas, on-loan striker Will Keane marked his home debut with the game's only goal when he drilled home from close range after 31 minutes.

BOLTON WANDERERS 1 IPSWICH TOWN 2

On-loan frontman Collin Quaner fired home a brace to give Town a first away win under the management of Paul Lambert as the Tractor Boys triumphed 2-1 at Bolton on 6 April 2019.

Quaner headed Lambert's men in front after 33 minutes and the travelling fans were given another opportunity to celebrate when he doubled Town's lead just before the interval. After being granted both time and space by the Wanderers' defence, Quaner fired in a right-footed effort from 20 yards then went in off an upright.

Despite some impressive attacking forays in the second period, Town were unable to add to their lead. An unfortunate own goal from Josh Emmanuel in injury time saw a nervy conclusion but Town held on for all three points.

IPSWICH TOWN 3 LEEDS UNITED 2

Town rounded off the 2018/19 season with a 3-2 Portman Road victory over Play-Off bound Leeds United after Collin Quaner struck in the 90th minute to ensure a difficult campaign ended on a winning note.

In front of a crowd of over 20,000 - Town opened the scoring through Flynn Downes after 30 minutes and really should have maintained their advantage until the break. However, Mateusz Klich levelled for the visitors on the stroke of half-time.

A thrilling second half began when Andre Dozzell fired Town back in front. Leeds equalised 14 minutes from time through Stuart Dallas and then saw Kemar Roofe fail to convert a penalty before Quaner had the final say.

Answer these questions on the 2018/19 campaign and see how much attention you were paying LAST SEASON!

1. Who made the most Championship appearances for the Blues last season?

ANSWER

2. Who was Town's first Championship win against last season?

ANSWER

3. How many points did Ipswich Town finish the 2018/19 season with?

ANSWER

4. How many times did Town draw in the Championship last season?

ANSWER

5. What was the highest home attendance of 2018/19?

ANSWER

6. Which five players received red cards last season?

ANSWER

7. Who did Town beat on the final day of the 2018/19 season?

ANSWER

8. How many Championship clean sheets did Dean Gerken keep last season?

ANSWER

9. Who received the most yellow cards last season?

ANSWER

10. Who came in on loan from Huddersfield Town in January 2019?

ANSWER

11. Who was the Blues first signing of summer 2018?

ANSWER

12. Who joint top scored last season with six Championship goals each?

ANSWER

ANSWERS ON PAGE 62

There are lots of exciting League One games ahead for the Tractor Boys in 2020 - here are three potential crackers...

FAST FORWARD

PETERBOROUGH UNITED (H)
1 February 2020

Ipswich start the busy month of February with a visit from regional rivals Peterborough United on Saturday, 1 February 2020.

This will be Posh's first visit to Portman Road since November 2012 when a DJ Campbell penalty secured Town a Championship point with a 1-1 draw.

The London Road outfit were big spenders in the summer and under the management of Darren Ferguson the club will have lofty ambitions for the 2019/20 campaign. This match could well have serious implications at the business end of the League One table, and with some local rivalry added to the mix, it is certainly one not to miss.

SUNDERLAND (A)
8 February 2020

Town's long trip to Sunderland's Stadium of Light on Saturday, 8 February 2020 will certainly be viewed as one of their biggest challenges of the League One season.

Following their relegation from the Championship in 2017/18, the Black Cats almost made an immediate return to the second tier but suffered the heartbreak of a Play-Off final defeat at the hands of Charlton Athletic.

Sunderland also suffered a Wembley defeat in the EFL Trophy final last season, Jack Ross and his players will therefore be aiming for automatic promotion come the conclusion of the 2019/20 season. Having amassed 85 points in League One last season, Sunderland know what the division is all about and will be aware of the importance of matches against fellow promotion contenders such as Ipswich.

PORTSMOUTH (H)
21 March 2020

Portsmouth ended last season just three points shy of the automatic promotion places before then falling at the semi-final stage of the League One Play-Offs.

EFL Trophy winners in 2018/19, Pompey are more than capable of performing on the big occasion and will be another club with aspirations of winning automatic promotion to the Championship in 2019/20.

Pompey's trip to Portman Road in March will be their first league game in Suffolk since they were beaten by a Keith Andrews goal at Championship level back in October 2011. The return of former Town striker Ellis Harrison, who joined the Fratton Park club in June 2019, will add some extra spice to the occasion.

PREMIER LEAGUE

OUR PREDICTION FOR PREMIER LEAGUE WINNERS:

MANCHESTER CITY

YOUR PREDICTION:

OUR PREDICTION FOR PREMIER LEAGUE RUNNERS-UP:

LIVERPOOL

YOUR PREDICTION:

CHAMPIONSHIP

OUR PREDICTION FOR CHAMPIONSHIP WINNERS:

MIDDLESBROUGH

YOUR PREDICTION:

OUR PREDICTION FOR CHAMPIONSHIP RUNNERS-UP:

LEEDS UNITED

YOUR PREDICTION:

LEAGUE ONE

OUR PREDICTION FOR LEAGUE ONE WINNERS:

IPSWICH TOWN

YOUR PREDICTION:

OUR PREDICTION FOR LEAGUE ONE RUNNERS-UP:

BLACKPOOL

YOUR PREDICTION:

FA CUP & EFL CUP

OUR PREDICTION FOR FA CUP WINNERS:

BOURNEMOUTH

YOUR PREDICTION:

OUR PREDICTION FOR EFL CUP WINNERS:

DERBY COUNTY

YOUR PREDICTION:

2020 PREDICTIONS

TEAMWORK

Every League One team is hidden in the grid, except one!

Can you figure out which is missing?

- AFC Wimbledon
- Accrington Stanley
- Blackpool
- Bolton Wanderers
- Bristol Rovers
- Burton Albion
- Bury
- Coventry City
- Doncaster Rovers
- Fleetwood Town
- Gillingham
- Ipswich Town
- Lincoln City
- Milton Keynes Dons
- Oxford United
- Peterborough United
- Portsmouth
- Rochdale
- Rotherham United
- Shrewsbury Town
- Southend United
- Sunderland
- Tranmere Rovers
- Wycombe Wanderers

ANSWERS ON PAGE 62

IPSWICH
MAGICAL
VEGAS
4
LUKE
CHAMBERS
IPSWICH TOWN
FOOTBALL CLUB

N

France international who joined Spurs from Olympique Lyonnais in July 2019

O

Rotherham winger signed from Brentford in August

P

League One club that knocked QPR out of this season's EFL Cup

Q

Ex-Hammer who made his debut for the Golden Boys last season

R

Scottish manager of the Black Cats

Joint Premier League top scorer last season alongside teammate Mané and Arsenal's Aubameyang

S

T

Nickname of Yorkshire club Barnsley

U

The Clarets' team kit manufacturer

V

The home of Championship new boys Charlton Athletic

A-Z

2019/20 PART 2

WHO'S WHO & WHAT'S WHAT OF ENGLISH FOOTBALL?

W Ipswich Academy graduate who spent last season on loan at Swindon Town

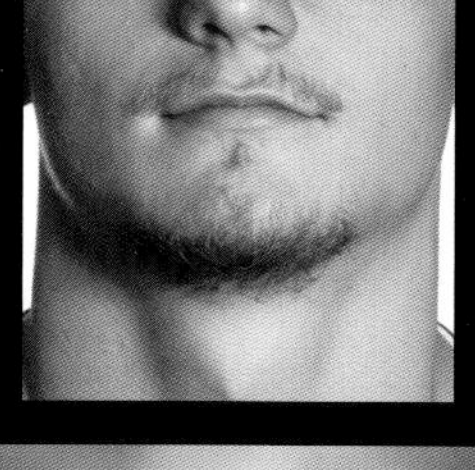

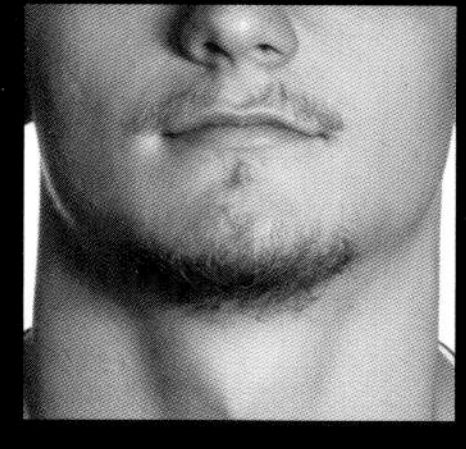

X Switzerland international who plays his home games at the Emirates Stadium

Y Nottingham Forest's Argentine defensive midfielder

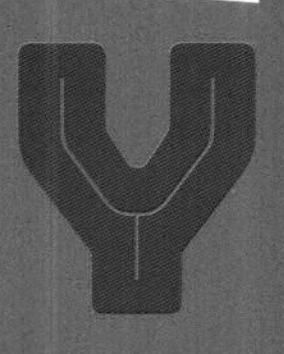

Z Hammers defender capped over 50 times by Argentina

ANSWERS ON PAGE 62

Freddie **SEARS** 20

POSITION: Striker **COUNTRY:** England **DOB:** 27 November 1989

Former West Ham United and Colchester frontman Freddy Sears smashed home a stunning long-range effort in Town's match away to Aston Villa in January that was voted Town's Goal of the Season. Sadly two games later and Sears' season came to an abrupt end when he suffered a cruciate ligament injury following a tackle with Norwich's Tom Trybull in Town's 3-0 defeat at Carrow Road. It is anticipated that Sears will return to action in the latter stages of 2019.

Flynn **DOWNES** 21

POSITION: Midfielder **COUNTRY:** England **DOB:** 20 November 1999

England youth international midfielder Flynn Downes is another member of the Town squad who has progressed from the club's academy to the first team. The all-action midfielder's committed performances have won him many admirers among the Town fanbase. He made 30 appearances in Town's 2018/19 Championship campaign and netted his first goal for the club in the final day victory over Leeds United.

Toto
NSIALA
22

POSITION: Defender **COUNTRY:** Congo DR **DOB:** 25 March 1992

Defender Toto Nsiala began his career with Premier League Everton and gained a growing reputation as a reliable defender in the Football League. Following stints with Accrington, Grimsby Town and Shrewsbury Town, Nsiala joined teammate Jon Nolan in following Shrews' boss Paul Hurst to Portman Road. A goal and a harsh red card in Town's away match with Sheffield Wednesday in August 2018 proved an eventful afternoon for Toto who made 24 appearances for Town in his debut season.

Andre
DOZZELL
23

POSITION: Midfielder **COUNTRY:** England **DOB:** 2 May 1999

Yet another product of Town's famed youth academy, Andre Dozzell is the son of former Ipswich star Jason. After marking his first team debut with a goal aged just 16, Dozzell's progress has been hampered by a number of injury setbacks. However, he featured regularly in Town squads under new boss Paul Lambert and will be looking to earn a first team starting slot in Town's 2019/20 League One campaign.

THE TEAM 2019/20

IPSWICH TOWN
FOOTBALL CLUB

CLUB
MAGICAL VEGAS

MAGICAL
VEGAS
2
JANOI
DONACIEN
IPSWICH TOWN
FOOTBALL CLUB

THE LEGEND KIERON DYER

Kieron Dyer progressed through the youth ranks at Portman Road and realised his dream of playing first team football for his local team. Dyer's senior debut came on Boxing Day 1996, just three days before his 18th birthday, as Town defeated Crystal Palace 3-1. The highly talented midfielder replaced Mick Stockwell for the final four minutes at Portman Road and his professional career was up and running.

After breaking into the Town first team in 1996/97, Dyer stepped up to become a first team regular in the 1997/98 campaign. The youngster wasted little time in making his mark on the season as he netted his first goal for the club in a First Division match away to Bradford City in August 1997.

Ipswich-born Dyer enjoyed one of his most satisfying afternoon's in a Town shirt when he played the club's memorable 5-0 victory over-arch rivals Norwich City on 21 February 1998. As a boyhood Town fan, Dyer cherished every minute of this Alex Mathie-inspired East Anglian derby triumph.

A superb 1997/98 season for Dyer saw him named in the PFA's First Division Team of the Year. In what was his first full season in the first team, Dyer featured in 51 fixtures for Town as the club reached the end-of-season First Division Play-Offs.

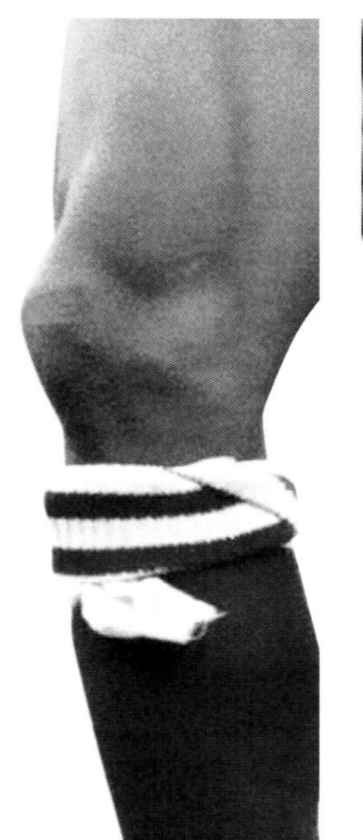

Despite Town ultimately suffering a third consecutive Play-Off semi-final defeat at the end of the 1998/99 season, Kieron Dyer starred in the thrilling second leg against Bolton Wanderers at Portman Road. He scored twice in the second-half to force extra-time as Town won the match 4-3 but missed out on Wembley on the away goals rule after the two legs ended 4-4.

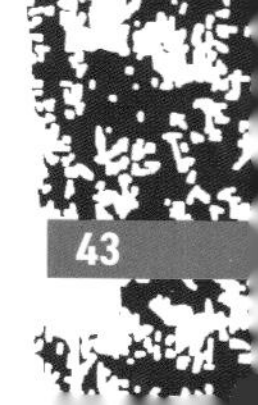

IPSWICH TOWN
HEY REF!
Do you always know what the officials are signalling?
Take a look at these and see if you are up to the job...
1
2
3
4

ANSWERS ON PAGE 62

THE 2019/20 SQUAD

Kane VINCENT-YOUNG 24

POSITION: **Defender** COUNTRY: **England** DOB: **15 March 1996**

Promising right-back Kane Vincent-Young joined Town in August 2019 following a switch from local rivals Colchester United. The defender started the season with the Us before signing for Town and making his Ipswich debut in the 5-0 romp away to Bolton Wanderers. His arrival at Portman Road will provide great competition for Town's right-back position.

Idris EL MIZOUNI

POSITION: **Midfielder** COUNTRY: **Tunisia** DOB: **29 September 2000**

Teenage midfielder Idris El Mizouni progressed through the academy Under-18 and Under-23 sides in 2018/19 to make his first team debut for Town in the 1-1 draw away to Play-Off chasing Bristol City in March 2019. He made a further three Championship appearances as the campaign drew to a close. His elevation to the Town first team resulted in an international debut for Tunisia in June 2019. El Mizouni's appearance in a friendly with Iran saw him become Town's first Tunisian international.

Luke WOOLFENDEN 28

POSITION: Defender **COUNTRY:** England **DOB:** 21 October 1998

Ipswich-born defender Luke Woolfenden will be looking to establish himself on the first team scene at Portman Road in 2019/20. With the ability to operate at either full-back or in a central role, Woolfenden progressed from the academy to make his professional debut at the end of the 2017/18 campaign. Following a substitute appearance in the opening day draw with Blackburn Rovers last season, Woolfenden then spent the 2018/19 campaign on loan with League Two Swindon Town where he made 36 appearances for the Robins.

Luke GARBUTT 29

POSITION: Defender **COUNTRY:** England **DOB:** 21 May 1973

Town agreed a season-long loan for highly-rated Everton left-back Luke Garbutt in July 2019, with the defender then linking up with his new teammates during the club's pre-season tour of Germany. With flexibility that enables him to perform at left-back or in a more advanced role on the left flank, Garbutt's ability to deliver the ball from wide areas is sure is be a useful weapon in the Blues' League One campaign.

THE LEGEND MATT HOLLAND

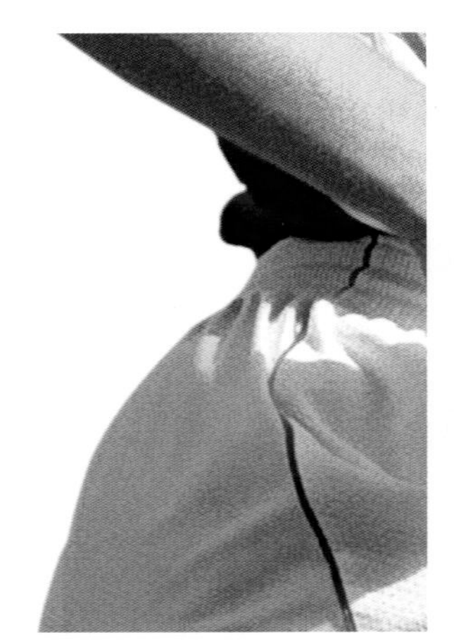

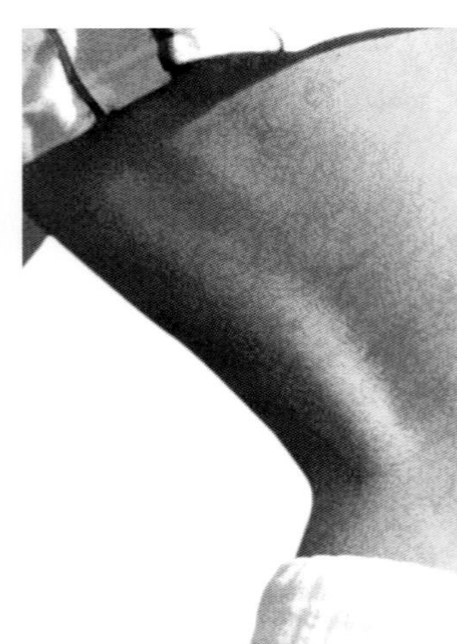

Midfield maestro Matt Holland made an immediate impression at Portman Road following his £800,000 transfer from Bournemouth in 1997. Holland chipped in with twelve goals in all competitions from midfield in 1997/98 and ended his first season at Portman Road by landing the club's Player of the Year award as Town reached the Division One Play-Offs.

Portman Road erupted when Matt Holland netted his second and Town's fourth goal of the night in the epic 1998/99 Play-Off semi-final second leg with Bolton Wanderers. Holland's goal came four minutes from the end of extra-time and put Town 4-3 ahead on the night and squared the tie at 4-4. Despite a ferocious backing from the stands in those minutes, Town could not grab a winner from what was a thrilling affair.

After twice suffering Play-Off semi-final defeats with Ipswich Town, it was a case of third time lucky for Holland and his teammates as promotion was secured in 1999/2000. After helping Town overcome Bolton Wanderers in the semi-final, Holland starred in the Town engine-room at Wembley as George Burley's side defeated Barnsley 4-2 and sealed promotion to the Premier League.

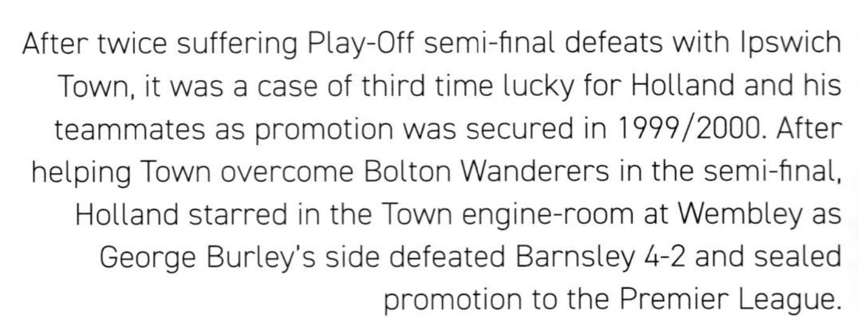

Such was Holland's club form while at Portman Road that the all-action midfielder received international recognition with the Republic of Ireland. He made his international debut for the Republic in 1999 and netted his first international goal during his fifth game against Portugal on 7 October 2000 in a World Cup qualifier.

Following Town's promotion to the Premier League via the 1999/2000 Play-Offs, Holland finally got to show his talents at the highest level. His growing reputation as a goalscoring midfielder was enhanced further when he netted his first Premier League goal in Town's 2-0 victory over Charlton Athletic on 11 November 2000.

8
COLE SKUSE
IPSWICH TOWN
FOOTBALL CLUB
MAGICAL
VEGAS

IPSWICH TOWN
FOOTBALL CLUB
There are five Ipswich stars hidden in the crowd, can you find them all?
FANTASTIC
32Red 32Red 32Red

ANSWERS ON PAGE 62

LUKE CHAMBERS

2018/19

PLAYER OF THE SEASON

Following the conclusion of what was a difficult season for all concerned at Portman Road, the club's loyal supporters voted skipper Luke Chambers their Player of the Year for 2018/19.

The Town captain pooled 29 per cent of the vote with two of the club's loan stars taking the second and third spots in the end-of-season poll. Everton loanee Matthew Pennington took the runners-up spot while Chelsea youngster Trevor Chalobah came third.

Chambers, who featured in 43 of Town's 46-game Championship programme in 2018/19, was often praised by new boss Paul Lambert for his commitment and leadership qualities in testing circumstances. The skipper put pen to paper on a new contract in the closing weeks of the season and will be as determined as anyone to help the club return to the Championship as soon as possible.

After receiving the Harwich Rosebow at the club's end-of-season awards event, Chambers paid tribute to the club's supporters who had stuck by the players during an ill-fated campaign.

"It's not the ideal situation to receive the award but all I can say is thanks to everyone that voted. It's a nice thing to receive but it's not the circumstances I'd want to receive it. I don't think there's really anyone that massively deserves the Player of the Year award.

"Obviously you guys probably should have got an award at some point for the support you've given us.

"It's been a frustrating time, but we've got a good group of players, good staff behind us and we'll crack on."

The end-of-season awards presentation event also saw all 16 of the club's 2018/19 debutants each presented with a silver salver to mark the beginning of their Town careers.

YOUNG PLAYER OF THE SEASON

JACK LANKESTER

Jack Lankester capped off a memorable season that saw him break through to the Town first team, by landing the Dale Roberts Academy Player of the Year award for 2018/19.

The exciting forward, who has been at the Ipswich Academy since the age of six, made eleven Championship appearances and added his name to the Town scoresheet in the New Year's Day match against Millwall.

With a big emphasis on young players stepping up to the Town first team, Lankester will be hopeful of further opportunities to showcase his talents at Portman Road in 2019/20.

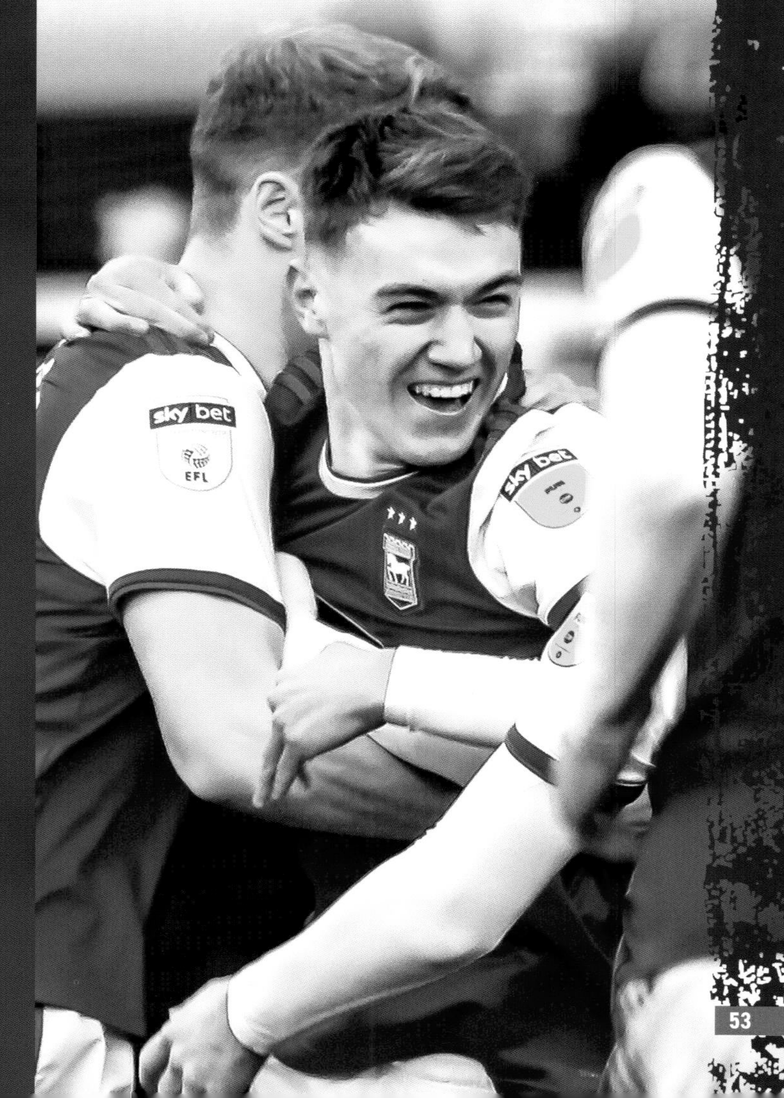

Myles KENLOCK 30

POSITION: Defender **COUNTRY:** England **DOB:** 26 November 1996

Defender Myles Kenlock agreed a new three-year contract at Portman Road in July 2019 after impressing Town boss Paul Lambert in the latter stage of the previous campaign. Having progressed from academy scholar to first team regular, Kenlock will be looking to become one of the first names on the manager's team sheet as Town bid to return to the second tier of English football as soon as possible.

THE 2019/20 SQUAD

Corrie NDABA 32

POSITION: Defender **COUNTRY:** Republic of Ireland **DOB:** 25 December 1999

A product of the Town Academy, powerful central defender Corrie Ndaba agreed a three-and-a-half-year professional contract with Town in February 2019. An impressive performer for Town at both Under-18 and Under-23 level, he has been capped by the Republic of Ireland at youth level. Ndaba will be keen to continue his development and push for a place in Paul Lambert's first team plans during the 2019/20 season.

Anthony
GEORGIOU 38

POSITION: MIDFIELDER **COUNTRY:** CYPRUS **DOB:** 24 February 1997

Town secured the loan signing of Cypriot international midfielder Anthony Georgiou from Tottenham Hotspur in August 2019, with the wideman agreeing a deal with Ipswich until January 2020. Well thought of at Spurs, Georgiou has already tasted Champions League football with the North London side. He made his Town debut as a substitute in the dramatic 2-1 home win over Wimbledon.

Emyr
HUWS 44

POSITION: Midfielder **COUNTRY:** Wales **DOB:** 30 September 1993

A talented box-to-box midfielder and full Welsh international, Emyr Huws joined Ipswich Town in the summer of 2017 following an impressive loan spell at Portman Road. Huws netted three goals from 13 appearances while on loan from Cardiff City and his permanent arrival was greeted with great approval by the Town fans. After a tough time with injuries everyone at Portman Road hopes to see the best of Huws in 2019/20.

WILL
KEANE 48

POSITION: STRIKER **COUNTRY:** England **DOB:** 11 January 1993

Striker Will Keane spent the second half of the 2018/19 season on loan at Portman Road from Hull City. He found the net three times in twelve outings for Town and certainly made a positive impression on both the club's management and supporters. After leaving the Tigers in the summer of 2019, he agreed a permanent one-year deal with Town as a free agent.

9
KAYDEN JACKSON
IPSWICH TOWN
FOOTBALL CLUB

Cover the wall in posters!
Portman Road
IPSWICH TOWN
FOOTBALL CLUB
Ipswich
IP1

The Tractor Boys have boasted a wealth of talent over the years! Here is our...

BLUES DREAM TEAM

...see if you agree!

GOALKEEPER

PAUL COOPER

Signed from Birmingham City in July 1971, goalkeeper Paul Cooper enjoyed FA Cup glory with Town in 1978 and UEFA Cup success in 1981. Cooper was renowned for his expertise at saving penalties.

YOUR CHOICE

FULL-BACK

GEORGE BURLEY

An FA Cup winner with Town in 1978, right-back George Burley won eleven Scotland caps while at Portman Road. After 394 league appearances for Ipswich, he later returned as managed and guided the club to the Premier League via the Play-Offs in 2000.

YOUR CHOICE

MIDFIELDER

JOHN WARK

A great Ipswich Town servant, attacking midfielder John Wark took in three playing spells at Portman Road. The heartbeat of Bobby Robson's team that enjoyed great success in the late 70s and early 80s, Wark also helped Town win the Second Division title in 1991/92.

YOUR CHOICE

MIDFIELDER

ARNOLD MUHREN

Dutch international midfielder Arnold Muhren arrived in Suffolk in 1978 and was Town's Player of the Year in 1978/79. A star performer in the club's 1981 UEFA Cup triumph, he scored 21 top-flight goals for Town before joining Manchester United.

YOUR CHOICE

MIDFIELDER

FRANS THIJSSEN

Frans Thijssen landed the Footballer of the Year accolade in 1981 as Town were crowned UEFA Cup winners. He followed fellow countryman Arnold Muhren to Ipswich and fans voted him their Player of the Year in 1979/80.

YOUR CHOICE

FULL-BACK

MILLS
3

MICK MILLS

Ipswich Town's record appearance maker, full-back Mick Mills captained the Blues to their FA Cup and UEFA Cup triumphs in 1978 and 1981. A full England international, Mills was ever-present in seven league campaigns during his lengthy Town career.

YOUR CHOICE

DEFENDER

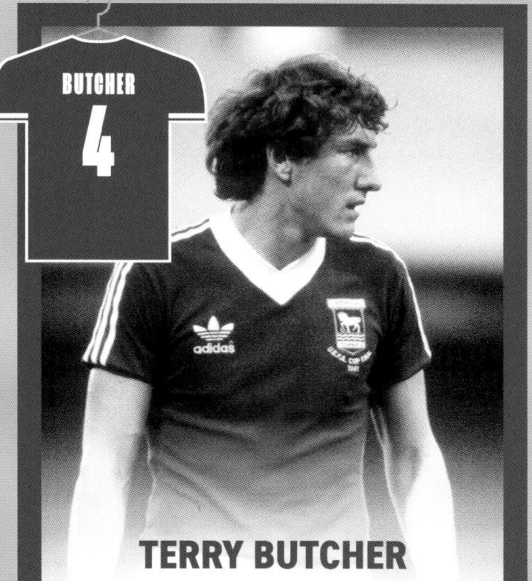

TERRY BUTCHER

Terry Butcher was a colossal force at the heart of the Ipswich defence. The England international formed an excellent partnership alongside Russell Osman and starred in the club's 1981 UEFA Cup triumph.

YOUR CHOICE

DEFENDER

KEVIN BEATTIE

Widely regarded by supporters as Ipswich Town's greatest ever player, Kevin Beattie was Player of the Year at Portman Road in consecutive seasons. An FA Cup winner in 1978, Beattie sadly passed away in September 2018.

YOUR CHOICE

FORWARD

PAUL MARINER

Striker Paul Mariner won 33 caps for England during a glittering Portman Road career. Signed from Plymouth Argyle in 1976, Mariner was Town's leading marksman in three consecutive seasons and a vital member of the FA Cup and UEFA Cup winning sides.

YOUR CHOICE

FORWARD

CRAWFORD
10

RAY CRAWFORD

England international Ray Crawford was Ipswich Town's top scorer as the club won the Second and First Division titles in consecutive seasons in 1960/61 and 1961/62. A key performer under the management of Alf Ramsey, he later played for Wolves and West Brom before returning to Town in 1966.

YOUR CHOICE

MIDFIELDER

CLIVE WOODS

Skilful winger Clive Woods was Man of the Match in Town's 1978 FA Cup final triumph over Arsenal. He initially turned professional at Portman Road in 1969 and was a member of the Ipswich team that mounted successive title challenges in the 70s.

YOUR CHOICE

TOP 10

MY TOP 10...

MOMENTS OF THIS YEAR

1.
2.
3.
4.
5.
6.
7.
8.
9.
10.

MY TOP 10...

FOOTBALLERS OF ALL TIME

1.
2.
3.
4.
5.
6.
7.
8.
9.
10.

MY TOP 10...

IPSWICH TOWN MEMORIES

1.
2.
3.
4.
5.
6.
7.
8.
9.
10.

MY TOP 10...

RESOLUTIONS FOR 2020

1.
2.
3.
4.
5.
6.
7.
8.
9.
10.

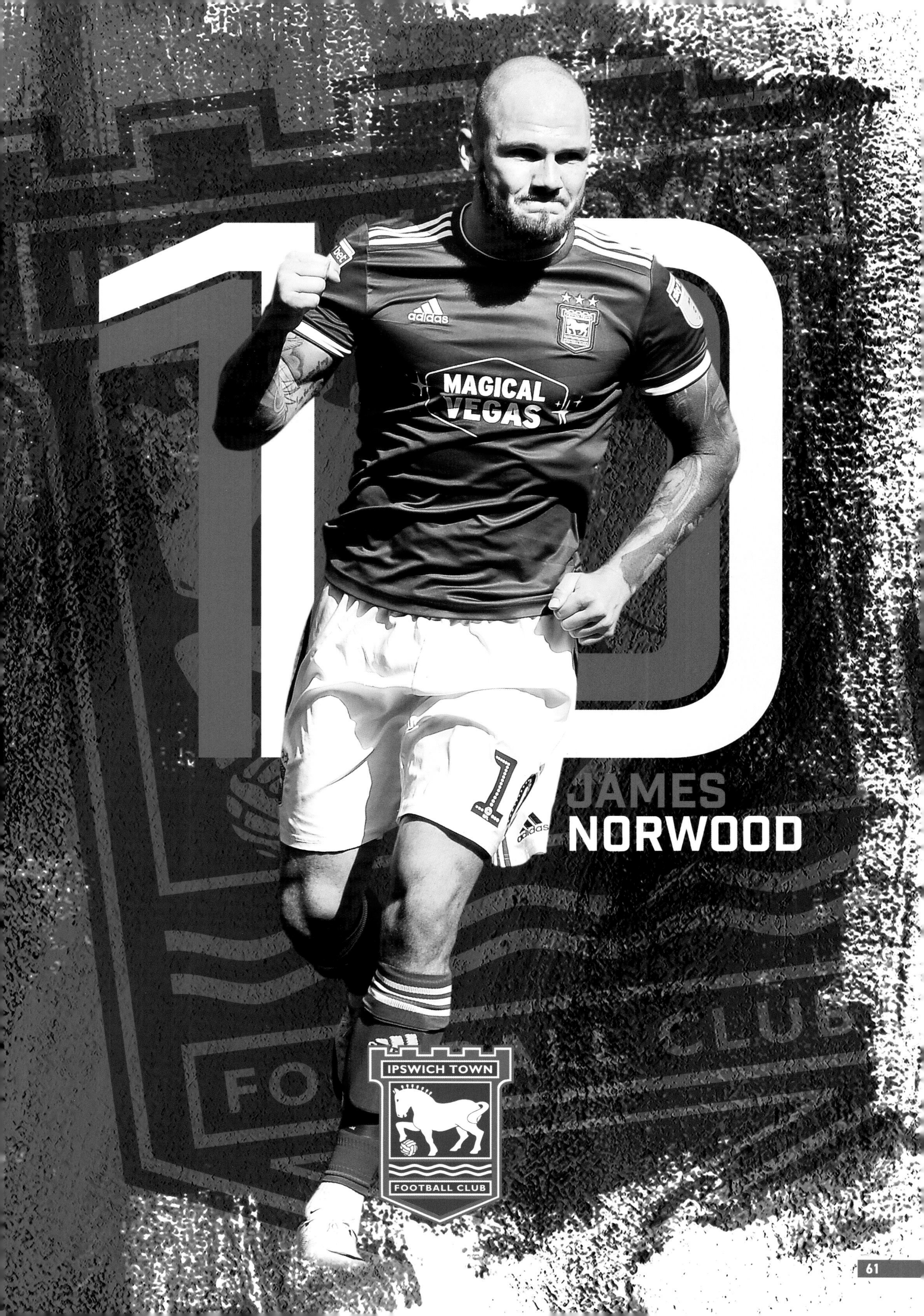
10
JAMES
NORWOOD
MAGICAL
VEGAS
adidas
IPSWICH TOWN
FOOTBALL CLUB

ANSWERS

PAGE 14 · A-Z PART ONE

A. César Azpilicueta. B. Burton Albion. C. Matty Cash. D. Harlee Dean. E. The Eagles. F. Lee Frecklington, Lincoln City. G. Goodison Park. H. Neil Harris. I. Kelechi Iheanacho. J. Gabriel Jesus. K. Mateusz Klich. L. Jesse Lingard. M. Darren Moore.

PAGE 24 · WHO ARE YER?

1. Toto Nsiala. 2. Luke Chambers. 3. Gwion Edwards. 4. Kayden Jackson. 5. Jack Lankester. 6. Idris El Mizouni. 7. Janoi Donacien. 8. Jon Nolan. 9. Teddy Bishop. 10. Myles Kenlock. 11. Will Norris. 12. James Norwood. 13. Cole Skuse. 14. Flynn Downes.

PAGE 31 · REWIND

1. Luke Chambers, 43 appearances. 2. Swansea City, 3–2, 6 October 2018. 3. 31 points. 4. 16. 5. 25,690 vs Norwich City, 2 Sep 2018. 6. Luke Chambers, Aristote Nsiala, Jonas Knudsen, Matthew Pennington and Tayo Edun. 7. Leeds United. 8. Three. 9. Luke Chambers, eight yellow cards. 10. Collin Quaner. 11. Matthew Healy. 12. Gwion Edwards and Freddie Sears.

PAGE 34 · TEAMWORK

Bolton Wanderers.

PAGE 36 · A-Z PART TWO

N. Tanguy Ndombele. O. Chiedozie Ogbene. P. Portsmouth. Q. Domingos Quina. R. Jack Ross, Sunderland. S. Mo Salah. T. The Tykes. U. Umbro. V. The Valley. W. Luke Woolfenden. X. Granit Xhaka. Y. Claudio Yacob. Z. Pablo Zabaleta.

PAGE 44 · HEY REF

1. Direct free kick. 2. Indirect free kick. 3. Yellow card - Caution. 4. Red card - Sending off. 5. Obstruction. 6. Substitution. 7. Offside/foul. 8. Penalty. 9. Offside location. 10. Play on.

PAGE 50 · FANTASTIC

Cole Skuse, Luke Chambers, Janoi Donacien, Jon Nolan and Teddy Bishop.